Linux Kernel Guide Book

The Basics of Linux Kernel Development

By William Rowley

Table of Contents

Disclaimer

While all attempts have been made to verify the information provided in this book, the author does assume any responsibility for errors, omissions, or contrary interpretations of the subject matter contained within. The information provided in this book is for educational and entertainment purposes only. The reader is responsible for his or her own actions and the author does not accept any responsibilities for any liabilities or damages, real or perceived, resulting from the use of this information.

The trademarks that are used are without any consent, and the publication of the trademark is without permission or backing by the trademark owner. All trademarks and brands within this book are for clarifying purposes only and are the owned by the owners themselves, not affiliated with this document. **

Introduction

Linux is a widely used operating system. The good thing with Linux is that it comes in a number of distributions, which are able to provide you with any kind of functionality which you may expect from an operating system. Each distribution is designed and developed so that it can help the target users to perform their tasks. The Linux kernel is the part of the Linux operating system which communicates directly with the computer hardware.

This is the part of the Linux operating system which one can edit so that they can have a customized operating system capable of meeting your personal or business needs. In most cases, Linux distributions are used in production environments It is good for you to know that the requirements for different businesses are also different.

The Linux development team understands this, and that is why they allow us to customize the kernels for their distributions. This calls for one to learn how to work with the Linux kernel. This book guides you in this, and you are guided in a step-by-step manner. Most of the kernel aspects, including the tools for its development are cussed. Enjoy reading!

Chapter 1- Initial RAM Disk (initrd)

The initrd provides us with a way of loading the RAM disk by use of the boot loader. After that, it becomes possible to mount the RAM disk to be the root file system, and we will be in a position to run programs from it. We can then mount a new root file system, particularly from another device. The previous root which was from the initrd will then be moved to a directory from which we can unmount it.

The initrd has been designed so that it can allow for system startup to happen only in two phases, in which the kernel will come up with a set of pre-compiled drivers, and any additional modules will have to be loaded from the initrd.

When the initrd is being used, the boot process takes the following sequence of steps:

1.   Boot loader loads kernel and initial RAM disk.

2. Kernel converts the initrd into a "normal" RAM disk, and then frees the memory which is used by the initrd.

3. If the sroot device is not the /dev/ram0, then the old (deprecated) change_root procedure will be followed.

4. The root device is mounted. In case it is /dev/ram0, then the initrd image will be mounted as the root.

5. The /sbin/init will be executed. It can be a valid executable, such as shell scripts, and it is executed with a uid of 0 and it can do everything the init can do.

6. The init then mounts "real" root file system.

7. The init places the root file system at the root directory by use of the pivot_root system call.

8. The init execs /sbin/init on our new root filesystem, so as to perform the usual boot sequence.

9. initrd file system will then be removed.

It is good for you to remember that once you change the root directory, you will not have to unmount it. This makes it possible for you to leave the processes running on the initrd during the procedure. Also, note that the file systems which are mounted under the initrd will always be accessible.

The Boot command-line Options

The following are some of the options for the initrd:

1. initrd=<path>   (e.g. LOADLIN)

    For loading a specified file as an initial RAM disk. When you are using LILO, you should specify a RAM disk image file in the /etc/lilo.conf file by use of the INITRD configuration variable.

2. Noinitrd

The initrd data is preserved without converting it to a RAM disk and a "normal" root file system is then mounted. The initrd data may be read from the /dev/initrd. Note that data in the initrd may have any structure, and it does not have to necessarily be a file system image. The option is mainly used for debugging. The /dev/initrd is read-only, and one can use it only once. Once the last process is closed, all the data will be freed, and the /dev/initrd will not be opened anymore.

root=/dev/ramo

The initrd is mounted as the root, and the normal boot procedure will be followed, with the RAM disk mounted as the root.

Compressed cpio Images

The recent kernels are capable of supporting the population of the Ramdisk from the compressed cpio archive. In such cases, the creation of a ramdisk image doesn't have to involve special block devices or loopbacks, you only have to create a directory on the disk with the initrd content which you need, change the directory by use of the cd command to that directory, and then execute the following command:

find . | cpio --quiet -H newc -o | gzip -9 -n > /boot/imagefile.img

For you to see the contents of a particular image in existence, you only have to do the following:

mkdir /tmp/imagefile

cd /tmp/imagefile

gzip -cd /boot/imagefile.img | cpio -imd –quiet

We began by making the directory by use of the "mkdir" command. We then changed to that directory, and then unzipped the image.

Installation

We should begin by creating a directory for the initrd, and this should be done in the "normal" root file system. The creation of the directory should be done by use of the mkdir command as shown below:

 # mkdir /initrd

In case the root file system had been created during the boot procedure, the procedure for creating the root file system should give the /initrd directory.

In some cases, the initrd will not be mounted, and it will be accessible in case the following device had been created:

 # mknod /dev/initrd b 1 250

 # chmod 400 /dev/initrd

Also, you have to compile the RAM disk support, and support for the initial disk RAM has to be enabled. All the components are in need of executing their programs from the initrd, which means that they must first be compiled into the kernel.

You should also create a RAM disk image. For you to do this, you have to create a file system on the block device, copy files to it as you need, and copy content of block device to the initrd file. The recent kernels allow this to be done with the following three devices:

- a floppy disk- but this may be slow.

- a RAM disk- this is fast, and it allocates a physical memory.

- a loopback device- this forms the best solution.

The loopback device method takes the following sequence of steps:

1. Make sure you have configured the loopback block devices into the kernel.

2. Create an empty file sy

3. Stem of any size that you need. An example of this is shown below:

 # dd if=/dev/zero of=initrd bs=300k count=1

 # mke2fs -F -m0 initrd

4. Mount your file system. This is shown below:

 # mount -t ext2 -o loop initrd /mnt

5. You can then go ahead to create some console device. This is shown below:

 # mkdir /mnt/dev

 # mknod /mnt/dev/console c 5 1

6. You can then properly copy all of the files which are necessary for the initrd to be used. The most important file of all these is the /sbin/init, and it should not be forgotten.

7. It will be possible for us to test the initrd environment without having to reboot, by use of the following command:

 # chroot /mnt /sbin/init

However, this only applies to initrd systems which are not able to interfere with the general state of the system.

8. You can then use the following command so as to unmount the file system:

 # umount /mnt

9. The initrd should now be in the file "initrd," and you can compress it optionally by use of the following command:

 # gzip -9 initrd

Finally, the kernel should be rebooted, and the initrd loaded. The majority of the Linux boot loaders are in support of initrd. The boot process at this point is compatible with the old mechanism, and that is why you have to pass the following command line parameters:

root=/dev/ram0 rw

The rw should only be used if we are writing to the initrd file system. With the LOADLIN, you just have to execute the following:

LOADLIN <kernel> initrd=<disk_image>

The following example demonstrates how you can do this:

LOADLIN C:\LINUX\BZIMAGE
initrd=C:\LINUX\INITRD.GZ root=/dev/ram0 rw

With LILO, the option "INITRD=<path>" has to be added to the global section or to a section of the respective kernel in the /etc/lilo.conf, and then the rest of the options can be passed by use of APPEND. This is shown in the example given below:

image = /bzImage

  initrd = /boot/initrd.gz

  append = "root=/dev/ramo rw"

You can then run the /sbin/lilo. At this point, you will be in a position to load and then enjoy using the initrd.

How to Change the Root Device

Once the init is done with its tasks, it usually changes the root device, and then goes ahead so as to start the Linux system on a "real" root device.

The following steps are followed:

- Mounting of a new root file system.

- Turning this into a root file system.

- Removing all the accesses to the initrd (old) root file system.

- Unmounting the initrd file system, and then de-allocating the RAM disk.

The process of mounting a new root file system should not be hard. The only thing to be considered is that the mounting should be done in a directory which is under our current root. Consider the example given below:

mkdir /new-root

mount -o ro /dev/hda1 /new-root

Root change is always done by use of a system call known as "pivot_root," and this can also be accessed through the pivot_root utility. It works by moving the current root to a directory which is under the root, and the new root is then put in place. The directory for the old root must be available before we can call the pivot_root. Consider the example given below:

cd /new-root

mkdir initrd

pivot_root . initrd

At this point, the init process will be in a position to access the old root through its executable, standard input/output/error, shared libraries, and the current root directory. The following command can then help you to release these references:

 # exec chroot . what-follows <dev/console >dev/console 2>&1

In the above command, "what-follows" represents a program located under the new root, which is /sbin/init. If you need to use the new root file system with udev, and there exists no valid /udev directory, the udev has to be initialized before we can invoke the chroot so as to provide /dev/console.

At this point, we can unmount the initrd and then free the memory which has been allocated by RAM. The following commands will help you do this:

 # umount /initrd

 # blockdev --flushbufs /dev/ramo

Also, feel free to use the intrd with a root which has been mounted with NFS.

Chapter 2- Kernel Development Tools

Kcov

This tool exposes the coverage information for the kernel code in a form which is suitable for coverage, that is, guided fuzzing. The coverage data for a running kernel is exposed through a kcov debugfs file. The coverage collection has to be enabled on the basis of an individual task, meaning that a single system call can be captured precisely.

Note that the aim of kcov is not to collect as much coverage as it can. Its function is to collect less or more coverage, which is a function of the syscall inputs. For it to achieve this concept, it doesn't have to collect coverage in hard/soft interrupts, and instrumentation of inherently non-deterministic parts will be disabled. The kernel can be configured as follows:

CONFIG_KCOV=y

This also needs a gcc which has been built on a revision which is not early than 231296. The profiling data will only be available after the debugfs has been mounted. This is shown below:

mount -t debugfs none /sys/kernel/debug

The following program is a demonstration of how the kcov can be used:

```
#include <stdio.h>
#include <stdint.h>
#include <fcntl.h>
#include <stdlib.h>
#include <stddef.h>
```

```c
#include <sys/types.h>

#include <sys/ioctl.h>

#include <sys/mman.h>

#include <sys/stat.h>

#include <unistd.h>


#define KCOV_INIT_TRACE            _IOR('c', 1, unsigned long)

#define KCOV_ENABLE         _IO('c', 100)

#define KCOV_DISABLE           _IO('c', 101)

#define COVER_SIZE      (64<<10)


int main(int argc, char **argv)
{
    int fd;
    unsigned long *cover, n, i;


    /* A single fd descriptor will allow coverage collection on some single
     * thread.
```

```
    */

fd = open("/sys/kernel/debug/kcov", O_RDWR);

if (fd == -1)

    perror("open"), exit(1);

/* Setup a trace mode and a trace size. */

if (ioctl(fd, KCOV_INIT_TRACE, COVER_SIZE))

    perror("ioctl"), exit(1);

/* Mmap buffer shared between the kernel- and the
user-space. */

cover = (unsigned long*)mmap(NULL, COVER_SIZE *
sizeof(unsigned long),

               PROT_READ | PROT_WRITE,
MAP_SHARED, fd, 0);

if ((void*)cover == MAP_FAILED)

    perror("mmap"), exit(1);

/* Enable coverage collection on current thread. */

if (ioctl(fd, KCOV_ENABLE, 0))

    perror("ioctl"), exit(1);

/* Reset coverage from the tail of the ioctl() call. */
```

```c
    __atomic_store_n(&cover[0], 0,
__ATOMIC_RELAXED);
    /* That is our target syscal call. */
    read(-1, NULL, 0);
    /* Read number of the PCs collected. */
    n = __atomic_load_n(&cover[0],
__ATOMIC_RELAXED);
    for (i = 0; i < n; i++)
        printf("0x%lx\n", cover[i + 1]);


    if (ioctl(fd, KCOV_DISABLE, 0))
        perror("ioctl"), exit(1);
    /* Free resources. */
    if (munmap(cover, COVER_SIZE * sizeof(unsigned
long)))
        perror("munmap"), exit(1);
    if (close(fd))
        perror("close"), exit(1);
    return 0;
}
```

Once this is piped through the addr2line, you will get the following result:

SyS_read

fs/read_write.c:562

___fdget_pos

fs/file.c:774

___fget_light

fs/file.c:746

___fget_light

fs/file.c:750

___fget_light

fs/file.c:760

___fdget_pos

fs/file.c:784

SyS_read

fs/read_write.c:562

If the program is in need of collecting the coverage from some several threads, then there will be an opening of /sys/kernel/debug/kcov in each of the threads, and this will be done separately. The interface being used is fine-grained, which is good for allowing forking of the test processes. A parent process will open the /sys/kernel/debug/kcov, then enable the mmaps coverage buffer, trace mode and it will then fork the child processes in a loop. The child processes may only have to enable the coverage.

Coccinelle

This is a tool used for pattern matching and for transforming text, and it has a number of uses in the development of the kernel, such as application of the tree-wide, complex patches as the names of the options which are used by the Coccinette files. This tool can be downloaded for any Linux distribution including Fedora, Ubuntu, Debian, OpenSUSE, Arch Linux. etc. Just open its page, and get the latest version.

Once this has been downloaded, run the command given below:

./configure

Make

The above command has been run as you are a regular user, and then the installation can be done as follows:

sudo make install

How to use it

The specific target for the coccinette is defined in top level Makefile. The target is given the name coccicheck, and it will call the coccicheck front-end which is located in the "scripts" directory.

There are four modes defined for this, and these include report, context, patch, and org. The model which is to be used is defined by setting of the mode variable using "MODE=<mode>." The following is a description of the above modes:

• patch specifies a fix, if possible.

• report will generate a list in the format: file:line:column-column: message.

• context selects the lines of interest as well as their context in a diff-like style. The lines of interest will be indicated with -.

• org will generate a report in Org mode format of the Emacs.

It is good for you to be aware that it is not all the patches that will be able to implement all the above modes. Note that the default mode has been set to "report," and this makes it easy for us to use the coccinelle. There are two other modes which provide us with a combination of the modes given above:

• chain will try the previous modes in the order above until one has succeeded.

• rep+ctxt will run the report mode successively and context mode. You should use it with the "C" option, which will check the code on a file basis.

If you need to create a report for each semantic patch, you have to run the command given below:

make coccicheck MODE=report

The patches can be produced by running the following command:

make coccicheck MODE=patch

The coccicheck target will apply each of the available semantic patches in the sub-directories of "scripts/coccinelle" to the whole of your Linux kernel.

For each of the semantic patches, a commit message will be proposed. It will give a description of the problem which is being checked by your semantic patch, and it will have a reference to your Coccinelle.

Similarly to the other static code analyzers, the Coccinelle always produces false positives. This means that you have to view the reports very carefully, and the patches should be reviewed.

Verbose messages can be enabled by setting of the V=variable as shown in the command given below:

make coccicheck MODE=report V=1

Coccinelle Parallelization

The default setting is that the coccinelle will try to run as parallel as it can. If you need to change this parallelism, you have to set the variable J=variable. A good example is when you need to run the parallelism across 3 cpus, as you can set the J variable to 3 as shown in the command given below:

make coccicheck MODE=report J=3

In Coccinelle 1.0.2, the Ocaml parmap is used for the purpose of parallelization. In case it is capable of supporting this, you will enjoy the benefit of parmap parallelization.

If you enable the parmap, the coccinelle will then enable the dynamic loading by use of the --chunksize 1 argument, and this will serve to ensure that we continue feeding the threads with the work one by one, and this will help us run away from a situation in which work will only be done by a few threads.

In the case of dynamic load balancing, if a thread has finished its work, then it will be fed with more work. If the parmap has been enabled, and an error has been detected in the Coccinelle, the error value will be propagated back, and the return value of the make coccicheck will capture the return value.

Coccinelle and Single Semantic Patch

The make variable COCCI which is optional can be used for making a single semantic patch. In such a case, the variable has to be initialized with a name for the semantic patch which will be applied. Consider this:

make coccicheck COCCI=<my_SP.cocci> MODE=patch

or

make coccicheck COCCI=<my_SP.cocci> MODE=report

Controlling Processing of Files

The default setting is that the entire kernel source tree stays checked. If you need to   enable the Cocinelle in a specific directory, you can use M=. If you need to check the drivers, you may write the following:

drivers/net/wireless/

If the Coccinelle is to be applied on the basis of a file, rather than on the basis of a directory, you can use the command given below:

make C=1 CHECK="scripts/coccicheck"

You can then check for the code which you have just edited. The value 2 should be applied to the C flag as shown below:

make C=2 CHECK="scripts/coccicheck"

In the modes, in which operations are done on a file basis, there exists no information regarding the semantic patches which are being displayed, and there will be no commit message which will be proposed.

In this case, each semantic patch will be run in the scripts/coccinelle by default. The COCCI variable may also be used to apply only a single semantic patch.

The default mode is the "report" mode. It is possible for you to use the MODE variable so as to select another mode.

How to Debug Coccinelle SmPL patches

The use of coccinelle is good, as options are provided in the spatch command line, and these options should match the ones we use when compiling the kernel. To know the meaning of these options, you can use the V=1, and then manually run the Coccinelle with the options for the debug enabled.

Alternatively, you may choose to debug the running Coccinelle against the SmPL patches by simply asking for stderr be redirected to stderr. Note that by default, the redirection of the stderr is done to the /dev/null, and if you need to capture it, you have to specify the option DEBUG_FILE="file.txt" to the coccicheck. This is shown below:

rm -f cocci.err

**make coccicheck
COCCI=scripts/coccinelle/free/kfree.cocci
MODE=report DEBUG_FILE=cocci.err**

cat cocci.err

The SPFLAGS can be used for the purpose of adding debugging flags, and you may have to add both –show-profile-trying to the SPFLAGS when you are debugging. You have to use the following:

rm -f err.log

export

COCCI=scripts/coccinelle/misc/irqf_oneshot.cocci

**make coccicheck DEBUG_FILE="err.log"
MODE=report SPFLAGS="--profile --show-trying"
M=./drivers/mfd/arizona-irq.c**

At this time, the err.log will have some profiling information, and the stdout will provide the progress information, as the Coccinelle will move forward with the work.

.cocciconfig support

The Coccinelle supports the reading of .cocciconfig by default. This is to know the options to be used each time a spatch is spawned. The variables in .cocciconfig take the following order of precedence:

- The current user's home directory has to be processed first.

- The directory from where the spatch is called has to be processed next.

- The directory provided with the −dir option has to be processed last, if it was used.

Since the coccicheck has to run through make, it has to run naturally from the kernel proper dir, and the second rule given above will be applied in picking up of the .cocciconfig when we are using the coccicheck.

The "make coccicheck" is also capable of supporting the use of M=targets In case you fail to supply any M=target, the assumption will be that you need to target the whole of the kernel.The coccicheck script for the kernel is as shown below:

if ["$KBUILD_EXTMOD" = ""] ; then

   OPTIONS="--dir $srctree $COCCIINCLUDE"
Else

   OPTIONS="--dir $KBUILD_EXTMOD
$COCCIINCLUDE"
Fi

The KBUILD_EXTMOD is always set once an explicit target is used with M=. In all of these cases, a spatch –dir argument will have to be usedmm since the third rule will have to be used whether or not you have used the M= option. In case the M= is not passed as an argument to the coccicheck, then the target directory will have to be the same as the directory from which we have called the patch.

If you are not using the coccicheck target of the kernel, the precedence given above should be kept in the order of .cocciconfig reading. If you are using the coccicheck target of the kernel, any .coccicheck's settings of the kernel should be overridden by use of the SPFLAGS.

The options which the coccinelle picks when it is reading the .cocciconfig will not appear as arguments to spatch the processes which are running in the system. If you need to confirm the options which are to be picked by the Coccinelle, just run the following command:

spatch --print-options-only

You can use your own index option so as to perform the override with SPFLAGS. If conflicts do occur with the available options, the Coccinelle will take precedence for the option which was passed last.

With .cocciconfig, it is easy for one to use idutils, but you must be given the order of precedence followed by the Coccinelle as the kernel has its own .cocciconfig, and the SPFLAGS has to be used if you need to use idutils.

The SPFLAGS variable also allows you to pass some additional options to the spatch. This will work as the Coccinelle is in respect for the last flags which are given to it once a conflict has occurred. The following command best describes this:

make SPFLAGS=--use-glimpse coccicheck

The Coccinelle is capable of supporting the idutils, but you must have coccinelle >= 1.0.6. In case you fail to specify an ID file, then the Coccinelle will assume that the ID database file is in the .id-utils.index file located on the top of the kernel. The coccinelle has a script named scripts/idutils_index.sh, and this uses the following to create the database:

mkid -i C --output .id-utils.index

In case you have some other database filename, you may have to symlink with it as shown below:

make SPFLAGS=--use-idutils coccicheck

You may also choose to give the database filename explicitly. The following demonstrates how this can be done:

**make   SPFLAGS="--use-idutils   /full-path/to/ID"
coccicheck**

If you need to know more regarding the spatch options, you can type "spatch –help."

Always remember that the "--use-idutils" and "--use-glimpse" options are in need of external tools which will be used for the purpose of indexing the code. This means that there comes none being active by default. However, if the code is indexed with one of the above tools, and based on the cocci file which has been used, then the spatch will be able to process the whole code base much quickly.

The "report" Mode in Detail

This mode usually gives a list in the format given below:

file:line:column-column: message

A good example is by running the following command:

make coccicheck MODE=report
COCCI=scripts/coccinelle/api/err_cast.cocci

The above will execute the following, which is just a part of the SmPL script:

<smpl>

@r depends on !context && !patch && (org || report)@

expression x;

position p;

@@

ERR_PTR@p(PTR_ERR(x))

```
@script:python depends on report@

p << r.p;

x << r.x;

@@


msg="ERR_CAST can be used with %s" % (x)

coccilib.report.print_report(p[0], msg)
</smpl>
```

The above will then show you some entries on the standard output, and these will be in the format given below:

/home/user/linux/crypto/ctr.c:188:9-16: ERR_CAST can be used with alg

/home/user/linux/crypto/authenc.c:619:9-16: ERR_CAST can be used with auth

/home/user/linux/crypto/xts.c:227:9-16: ERR_CAST can be used with alg

The "patch" Mode in Detail

If this mode is used, then it will have to specify a fix for any problem which may arise. A good example is when you run the following command:

make coccicheck MODE=patch COCCI=scripts/coccinelle/api/err_cast.cocci

This will in turn run the following part of SmLP script:

< smpl >

@ depends on !context && patch && !org && !report

@

expression x;

@@

- ERR_PTR(PTR_ERR(x))

+ ERR_CAST(x)

`</smpl>`

On your standard output, you will get some patch hunks in the format given below:

```
diff -u -p a/crypto/ctr.c b/crypto/ctr.c
--- a/crypto/ctr.c 2017-01-21 10:47:28.000000000 +0200
+++ b/crypto/ctr.c 2017-01-03 13:41:49.000000000 +0200
@@ -185,7 +185,7 @@ static struct crypto_instance *crypto_ct
   alg = crypto_attr_alg(tb[1], CRYPTO_ALG_TYPE_CIPHER,
               CRYPTO_ALG_TYPE_MASK);
   if (IS_ERR(alg))
-      return ERR_PTR(PTR_ERR(alg));
+      return ERR_CAST(alg);

   /* Block size must be >= 4 bytes. */
   err = -EINVAL;
```

The "context" Mode in Detail

This is for highlighting some lines of text which are needed as well as their context, and this is done in diff-like style. It is good for you to remember that the output which you get from this will not be an applicable patch. This mode just highlights the lines of interest, and the rest of the surrounding lines will be given some context. Suppose we run the command given below:

make coccicheck MODE=context
COCCI=scripts/coccinelle/api/err_cast.cocci

The following, which is a part of the SmLP script, will be executed:

<smpl>

@ depends on context && !patch && !org && !report@

expression x;

@@

* ERR_PTR(PTR_ERR(x))

</smpl>

You will have some diff hunks on standard output as shown below:

```
diff -u -p /home/user/linux/crypto/ctr.c
/tmp/nothing
--- /home/user/linux/crypto/ctr.c   2017-01-26
11:29:18.000000000 +0200

+++ /tmp/nothing

@@ -185,7 +185,6 @@ static struct crypto_instance
*crypto_ct

   alg = crypto_attr_alg(tb[1],

CRYPTO_ALG_TYPE_CIPHER,

                CRYPTO_ALG_TYPE_MASK);

   if (IS_ERR(alg))

-       return ERR_PTR(PTR_ERR(alg));
```

```
/* Block size must be >= 4 bytes. */

err = -EINVAL;
```

The "org" Mode

This mode is used for generating a report in Org mode format of the Emacs. A good example is when we run the following command:

**make coccicheck MODE=org
COCCI=scripts/coccinelle/api/err_cast.cocci**

The part for the SmLP script given below will then be executed:

<smpl>

@r depends on !context && !patch && (org || report)@

expression x;

position p;

@@

ERR_PTR@p(PTR_ERR(x))

@script:python depends on org@

p << r.p;

x << r.x;

@@

msg="ERR_CAST can be used with %s" % (x)

msg_safe=msg.replace("[","@(").replace("]",")")

coccilib.org.print_todo(p[0], msg_safe)

</smpl>

When the above is executed, Org entries will be generated on standard output. These will be in the format given below:

* TODO
[[view:/home/user/linux/crypto/ctr.c::face=ovl-

face1::linb= 188::colb=9::cole=16][ERR_CAST can be
used with alg]]

* TODO
[[view:/home/user/linux/crypto/authenc.c::face=ovl-
face1::linb=619::colb=9::cole=16][ERR_CAST can be
used with auth]]

* TODO
[[view:/home/user/linux/crypto/xts.c::face=ovl-
face1::linb=227::colb= 9::cole=16][ERR_CAST can be
used with alg]]

Chapter 3- Writing Linux Kernel Modules

In this chapter, we will be creating a Linux kernel module for an embedded Linux device.

A Loadable Kernel Module (LKM) refers to a mechanism by which you can add or remove code from a Linux kernel during runtime. This is ideal for the device drivers so that the kernel can be made to communicate with the hardware without the need of knowing how the hardware works. The KLM's alternative would be to create some code for each driver in the Linux kernel.

Without this, the Linux kernel would be too big, as we would have to create some support for each driver. We would also have to build the kernel any time that we needed to add some new hardware or update its device manager.

However, with LKMs, one must manage the driver files for all devices. The LKMs have to be loaded during the runtime, but they will not be loaded to the user space, since they are part of the kernel.

The kernel modules usually run in the kernel space, but the applications usually run in the user space. The user space and the kernel space have their own address space, and these do not overlap. This means that an application which is running in the user view will have a complete view of the hardware.

System Preparation

We should begin by preparing the system so as to build the kernel code, meaning that one must have the Linux headers readily installed on the Linux system. You can use the package manager on your typical Linux desktop so as to know the right package which you are to install. This calls for you to search for the appropriate Linux headers. For those running a 64-bit Debian, use the following sequence of steps:

```
$ sudo apt-get update
$ apt-cache search linux-headers-$(uname -r)
linux-headers-3.16.0-4-amd64 - Header files for
Linux 3.16.0-4-amd64
$ sudo apt-get install linux-headers-3.16.0-4-amd64
$ cd /usr/src/linux-headers-3.16.0-4-amd64/
$ ls
arch include Makefile Module.symvers scripts
```

In this case, the LKM has been built on BeagleBone, and the process will be made simpler as compared to cross-profiling. Note that the headers have to be installed for the correct Linux version. You can use uname so as to know the correct installation. You just have to type the following:

$ uname –a

It is now time for you to download Linux headers for the BeagleBone platform. You have to choose the exact kernel build, and then download and install the correct Linux headers. The following example best demonstrates this:

$ wget http://rcn-ee.net/deb/precise-armhf/v3.8.13-bone70/linux-headers-3.8.13-bo**ne70_1precise_armhf.deb**

$ sudo dpkg -i ./linux-headers-3.8.13-bone70_1precise_armhf.deb

If everything is okay, then the headers should have been installed. You can then use the command given below so as to verify whether or not the packages were installed:

$ cd /usr/src/linux-headers-3.8.13-bone70/

Module Code

The execution of a computer program is very straightforward. A loader is responsible for allocating some memory to the program, and then it loads the program, together with any libraries which are needed. There is some point at which the execution of instructions starts, and the program runs to the end. Once the program exits, the operating system will look for any memory leaks, and then frees any lost memory to pool.

A kernel module is not the same as an application. It has no main() function. It is good for you to know that the kernel modules are not executed sequentially. The kernel module has to register itself for handling requests by use of its initialization function, which will run and then terminate. The type of requests which can be handled have to be defined in the module code. This can be seen to be similar to the event-driven programming which is highly used in the graphical user interface (GUI) programming.

Also, there is no automatic cleanup in the kernel modules. This means that any resources which are allocated to the module will have to be released manually once the module is loaded, or they may end up being unavailable until the system has rebooted. The kernel modules usually have some high value in terms of privilege of execution.

This is because more cpu cycles have to be allocated to the kernel module as compared to the user programs. Although it is possible for the kernel modules to be interrupted, it is good for us to design them well, so that they can behave well once they have been interrupted. Consider the module code given below:

```
/**

 * @file   hello.c

  * @date 21 Jan 2017

 * @version 0.1

  * @brief  A "Hello World!" loadable kernel module
(LKM) which can display some message


 * in /var/log/kern.log file once the module has been
loaded and removed. The module is capable of
accepting an


 * argument once it has been loaded -- the name, that
appears in kernel log files.
```

```
*/

#include <linux/init.h>

// Macros for marking up functions example, __init
__exit

#include <linux/module.h>

// Core header to load the LKMs into the kernel

#include <linux/kernel.h>

// has macros, types, functions for the kernel


MODULE_LICENSE("GPL");

///< The license type – which will affect the runtime
behavior
MODULE_AUTHOR("Derek Molloy");

///< The author – will be visible once you use
modinfo
```

```
MODULE_DESCRIPTION("Soe simple Linux driver
for BBB.");
```

///< The description

```
MODULE_VERSION("0.1");     ///< The version of
your module
```

```
static char *name = "world";
```

///< An example LKM argument – its default value is

"world"

```
module_param(name, charp, S_IRUGO);
```

///< Param desc. charp = char ptr, S_IRUGO may be
read but not changed

```
MODULE_PARM_DESC(name, "The name which will
be displayed in /var/log/kern.log"); ///< parameter
description
```

```
/** @brief LKM initialization function
```

* The static keyword will restrict the visibility of function to within the C file. The __init

 * macro means for a built-in driver (but not a LKM) a function will only be used at the initialization

 * time and it can be discarded, its memory freed up.

 * @return will return 0 if it is successful

 */

```c
static int __init helloBBB_init(void){

    printk(KERN_INFO "EBB: Hello %s from BBB LKM!\n", name);


    return 0;

}
```

/** @brief LKM cleanup function

 * Just like the initialization function, this is static. The __exit macro will notify if this

```
* code has been used for some built-in driver (but
not a LKM) this function is not needed.



*/


static void __exit helloBBB_exit(void){

   printk(KERN_INFO "EBB: Goodbye %s from the
BBB LKM!\n", name);



}




/** @brief A module has to use the module_init()
module_exit() macros from the linux/init.h, which


* identifies the initialization function at the insertion
time and cleanup function (as


* listed above)

*/

module_init(helloBBB_init);

module_exit(helloBBB_exit);
```

For us to go ahead and then build the kernel module, we must have a Makefile. To be precise, this should be a special kbuild Makefile. The Makefile for the above kernel module is as shown below:

obj-m+=hello.o

all:

    make -C /lib/modules/$(shell uname -r)/build/ M=$(PWD) modules

clean:

    make -C /lib/modules/$(shell uname -r)/build/ M=$(PWD) clean

In the above Makefile, the first line is known as the goal definition, and it is used to define the module which is to be built. In this case, the module is hello.o. The syntax for this might be a bit complex, with the obj-m representing a loadable module goal, while obj-y is a representation of a built-in object goal. When you need to build a module from a number of objects, then the syntax will become somehow complex. However, we have what is enough to build this type of module.

The $(shell uname -r) is useful as it is a call for returning a current kernel build version, and this will make sure that some degree of portability exists for the Makefile. The use of the −C option will enable switching to a kernel directory before any tasks can be performed. The variable assignment for M=$(PWD) tells the Make command where there is the actual profile file.

The target for the module is the default target for the external kernel modules. Some alternative target is the "modules_install" which will install the module. Note that the make command should be installed with the superuser permissions, and the path for the module installation is needed.

If all goes well, the process necessary for creation of the kernel module has to be straight forward, and you only have to have installed the necessary kernel modules as we had stated earlier. The steps should involve the execution of the following series of commands:

```
$ ls –l
```

```
$ ls –l
```

```
$ ls
```

You will see that a hello loadable kernel module is available in the build directory, and this will have a file extension of .ko.

We can now use the kernel module tools so as to load this module. This can be done through the following sequence of commands:

$ ls -l *.ko

$ sudo insmod hello.ko

$ lsmod

$ modinfo hello.ko

$ sudo rmmod hello.ko

The steps can then be repeated and after that, view the output in the kernel log, and this will result from use of the printk() function.

It is recommended that you make use of a second terminal window for viewing the output as the KLM is being loaded and unloaded. This can be done as shown below:

```
$ sudo su -

# cd /var/log

# tail -f kern.log
```

The LKM custom parameter can now be tested. The code has a custom parameter, which is responsible for allowing an argument to be passed to the kernel module on initialization. You can use the following to test for the feature:

```
$ sudo insmod hello.ko name=John
```

Once you view the /var/log/kern.log at this time, you will see the text "Hello John" rather than "Hello world." It is good for you to have the /sys and /proc first.

Instead of using the lsmod command, it is possible for you to determine the information regarding the module which has been loaded. This is demonstrated below:

$ cd /proc

$ cat modules|grep hello

The information you get will be similar to that which you get from the lsmod command in addition to the provision of current kernel memory offset for the loaded module, and this is of importance when it comes to debugging.

The LKM also provides an entry under /sys/module. This will grant us a direct access to a custom parameter state. An example of this is given below:

```
$ cd /sys/module
$ ls -l|grep hello
$ cd hello
$ ls –l
$ cat version
$ cat taint
```

If you need to view the custom parameter, follow the steps given below:

```
$ cd parameters/
$ ls –l
$ cat name
```

You will get the result as "John," but if you used a different name, that is the one you will get. You will also realize that you were not expected to have the super user details so that you can view those details. In the latter case, we had used the S_IRUGO argument so as to define the module parameter.

This value can be configured for write access, but the module code will have to detect the state change and then react as expected. The module can then is removed, and then check for the output:

The following command can be used for this purpose:

$ sudo rmmod hello.ko

You will then get a message in the kernel logs.

 # tail -f kern.log

Character Device Drivers

A character device is used for transferring data to and from an application, they work like serial ports or pipes, and the data is written character-by-character. This chapter describes a straightforward character driver which can be used for passing information between a Linux user-space program and a loadable kernel module (LKM), running in a Linux kernel space.

The device drivers are associated with some major and minor numbers. A good example is the /dev/ram0 and the /dev/null which are associated with a driver with a major number 1, and the /dev/tty0 and the /dev/ttyS0 which are associated with a driver with a major number 4. The kernel usually makes use of the major number so as to identify the best device driver once the device has been accessed.

The usage of the minor number depends on the device which is being used, and this has to be handled internally by the driver. If you need to know the major and the minor number for each device, you have to navigate to the /dev directory and then perform the listing. This command given below can help you achieve this:

$ ls –l

The character devices are identified by use of the letter "c" in the first column after you have listed. You must have observed this. The block devices are identified by use of the letter "b." You must also have seen the permissions for access, the owner,and the group to which the device belongs. You can type the command given below:

$ groups

File Operations Data Structure

The file_operations is stored in /linux/fs.h, and it has the pointers to functions in a driver which allows one to define the behavior for some file operations. In this case, we are going to define implementation for read, write, open, and release, which are system call operations. If implementation for any one of these is not provided, then it will point to NULL and it will be inaccessible. This is shown in the following data structure:

// Note: __user is the user-space address.

struct file_operations {

struct module *owner;   // Pointer to LKM that owns the structure

loff_t (*llseek) (struct file *, loff_t, int);

// Change current read/write position in a file

ssize_t (*read) (struct file *, char __user *, size_t, loff_t *);

// For retrieving data from device

```
ssize_t (*write) (struct file *, const char __user *,
size_t, loff_t *);
```

// For sending data to device

```
ssize_t (*aio_read) (struct kiocb *, const struct iovec
*, unsigned long, loff_t); // an asynchronous read
```

```
ssize_t (*aio_write) (struct kiocb *, const struct
iovec *, unsigned long, loff_t); // Asynchronous write
```

```
ssize_t (*read_iter) (struct kiocb *, struct iov_iter
*);
```
 // possibly asynchronous read

```
ssize_t (*write_iter) (struct kiocb *, struct iov_iter
*);
```

// possibly asynchronous write

```
int (*iterate) (struct file *, struct dir_context *);
```

// called whenever the VFS is in need of reading
directory contents

```
unsigned    int    (*poll)    (struct    file    *,    struct
poll_table_struct *);
```

```
long (*unlocked_ioctl) (struct file *, unsigned int,
unsigned long); /
```

/ Called by ioctl system call

```
long (*compat_ioctl) (struct file *, unsigned int,
unsigned long);
```

// Called by ioctl system call

```c
int (*mmap) (struct file *, struct
vm_area_struct *);
```

// Called by the mmap system call

```c
int (*mremap)(struct file *, struct vm_area_struct
*);
```

// Called by the memory remap system call

```c
int (*open) (struct inode *, struct file *);
```

// first operation which is performed on the device file

```c
int (*flush) (struct file *, fl_owner_t id);
```

// called once the process has closed its copy of

descriptor

```c
int (*release) (struct inode *, struct file *);
```

// called when the file structure has been released

```c
int (*fsync) (struct file *, loff_t, loff_t, int datasync);
```

// notify device of the change in the FASYNC flag

```c
int (*aio_fsync) (struct kiocb *, int datasync);      //
```
synchronous notify device of change in its FASYNC flag

```c
int (*fasync) (int, struct file *, int);
```

// asynchronously notify the device of the change in the FASYNC flag

```c
int (*lock) (struct file *, int, struct file_lock *);
```

// used for implementing the file locking

...

};

The Source Code for a Device Driver

The drivers should have the class name and the device name. In the following example, the class name is "ebb" while "ebbchar" refers to the device name. With this, a file system will be created at "/sys/class/ebb/ebbchar." Here is the example:

```
#include <linux/init.h>

#include <linux/module.h>

#include <linux/device.h>

#include <linux/kernel.h>

#include <linux/fs.h>

#include <asm/uaccess.h>

#define  DEVICE_NAME "ebbchar"

#define  CLASS_NAME "ebb"
```

```c
MODULE_LICENSE("GPL");

MODULE_AUTHOR("Derek Molloy");

MODULE_DESCRIPTION("Simple Linux char driver
for BBB");

MODULE_VERSION("0.1");


static int   majorNumber;

static char  message[256] = {0};

static short size_of_message;

static int   numberOpens = 0;

static struct class* ebbcharClass  = NULL;

static struct device* ebbcharDevice = NULL;

static int   dev_open(struct inode *, struct file *);

static int   dev_release(struct inode *, struct file *);

static ssize_t dev_read(struct file *, char *, size_t,
loff_t *);

static ssize_t dev_write(struct file *, const char *,
size_t, loff_t *);

static struct file_operations fops =
```

```c
{
    .open = dev_open,

    .read = dev_read,

    .write = dev_write,

    .release = dev_release,
};
static int __init ebbchar_init(void){

    printk(KERN_INFO "EBBChar: Initializing
EBBChar LKM\n");


    majorNumber = register_chrdev(0,
DEVICE_NAME, &fops);

    if (majorNumber<0){

        printk(KERN_ALERT "EBBChar has failed to
register some major number\n");
        return majorNumber;

    }

printk(KERN_INFO "EBBChar: has registered
correctly with the major number %d\n",
majorNumber);


    ebbcharClass     =     class_create(THIS_MODULE,
CLASS_NAME);

    if (IS_ERR(ebbcharClass)){
```

```c
    unregister_chrdev(majorNumber,
DEVICE_NAME);

    printk(KERN_ALERT "Failed to register the device
class\n");

    return PTR_ERR(ebbcharClass);      =

}

    printk(KERN_INFO "EBBChar: device class has
registered correctly\n");


    ebbcharDevice = device_create(ebbcharClass,
NULL, MKDEV(majorNumber, 0), NULL,
DEVICE_NAME);

  if (IS_ERR(ebbcharDevice)){

    class_destroy(ebbcharClass);

    unregister_chrdev(majorNumber,

DEVICE_NAME);

    printk(KERN_ALERT "Failed to create device\n");

    return PTR_ERR(ebbcharDevice);

}

    printk(KERN_INFO "EBBChar: the device class was
created correctly\n");

  return 0;

}
```

```c
static void __exit ebbchar_exit(void){

  device_destroy(ebbcharClass,

MKDEV(majorNumber, 0));

  class_unregister(ebbcharClass);

  class_destroy(ebbcharClass);

  unregister_chrdev(majorNumber,

DEVICE_NAME);

  printk(KERN_INFO "EBBChar: Goodbye from LKM!\n");

}


static int dev_open(struct inode *inodep, struct file *filep){

  numberOpens++;

  printk(KERN_INFO "EBBChar: Device was opened %d time(s)\n", numberOpens);

  return 0;

}


static ssize_t dev_read(struct file *filep, char *buffer, size_t len, loff_t *offset){
```

```c
    int error_count = 0;

    error_count = copy_to_user(buffer, message,
size_of_message);

    if (error_count==0){         // if true it is success

        printk(KERN_INFO "EBBChar: Sent %d
characters to user\n", size_of_message);

        return (size_of_message=0);

    }

    else {

        printk(KERN_INFO "EBBChar: Failed to send %d
characters to user\n", error_count);

        return -EFAULT;

    }

}



static ssize_t dev_write(struct file *filep, const char
*buffer, size_t len, loff_t *offset){

    sprintf(message, "%s(%zu letters)", buffer, len);

// appending received a string with its length

    size_of_message = strlen(message);

// store length of stored message
```

```
    printk(KERN_INFO "EBBChar: Received %zu
characters from user\n", len);

    return len;

}


static int dev_release(struct inode *inodep, struct file

*filep){

    printk(KERN_INFO "EBBChar: Device was
successfully closed\n");

    return 0;

}

module_init(ebbchar_init);

module_exit(ebbchar_exit);
```

You can then go ahead so as to build the LKM. This can be done by use of a Makefile. This will build a user-space C program which will interact with the LKM. This is shown below:

obj-m+=ebbchar.o

```
all:

        make -C /lib/modules/$(shell uname -r)/build/
M=$(PWD) modules

        $(CC) testebbchar.c -o test

clean:

        make -C /lib/modules/$(shell uname -r)/build/
M=$(PWD) clean

        rm test
```

Conclusion

We have come to the end of this book. The Linux kernel is the one which is responsible for communicating directly with the computer hardware. It is a very useful part of the Linux system. You must have heard that Linux is an open source operating system. This means that you can download the Linux kernel and then edit it so that it can meet your needs. This is good; as it helps you customize the operating system so as to meet your needs.